P9-BXZ-009

Unless
We Pray

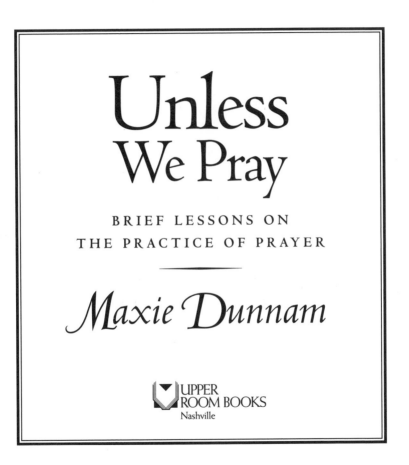

Unless
We Pray

BRIEF LESSONS ON
THE PRACTICE OF PRAYER

Maxie Dunnam

UPPER
ROOM BOOKS
Nashville

Cover Design: Gore Studio, Inc.
First Printing: January 1998

The Upper Room Web Site: http://www.upperroom.org

The Library of Congress Cataloging-in-Publication Data
Dunnam, Maxie D.
        Unless we pray: brief lessons on the practice of prayer/ Maxie Dunnam.
            p.   cm.
        ISBN 0-8358-0841-6 (hardback)
        I. Prayer—Christianity.   I. Title.
    BV210.2.D83   1998
    248.3'2—dc21   97-27913
                                                     CIP

Printed in the United States of America

To Jerry, my wife

A person who prays
is a person standing with open arms
to embrace the world
and all that is with the love of God.
She is that kind of person and I love her.

As prayer often seems absurd,
so her love for me—and I'm grateful.

Introduction

*What if God is as dependent upon
our praying as he is upon our acting? What if there
are some things God either cannot or will not do
until and unless we pray?*

There are some things God either cannot or will
not do *unless* people pray. Thus the title of this collection.
This and other brief lessons on the practice of prayer are
taken from books I have written and sermons I have
preached over the past twenty-five years.

It is my hope that because these lessons are brief,
you can put them into practice on the go. One way to do it
is to take one per day—memorize it, reflect on it often
during the day, and put it into practice during your prayer
times. Or use it as a conversation subject with friends.

You can read the book any way you please. You
may start on the first page or just open it wherever your

thumb guides you. You may read it as a daily spiritual discipline or keep it by your favorite chair, or in the bathroom, or on the kitchen table where you can open and read at random. You do not have to read much at a time . . . three or four lessons at the most. Though brief, these are important, even profound lessons, that you need to reflectively "chew on" in order to put them into practice.

My prayer is that these lessons will move you from *until* and *unless* to *now and always* in praying daily and in a disciplined way, until praying becomes spontaneous and all of life is prayer.

*Some quotations in this volume are from *Barefoot Days of the Soul* (© 1975 by Word, Incorporated; Upper Room edition), and the following Maxie Dunnam workbooks published by Upper Room Books: *The Workbook of Living Prayer* (© 1974), *The Workbook of Intercessory Prayer* (© 1979), and *The Workbook on Spiritual Disciplines* (© 1984).

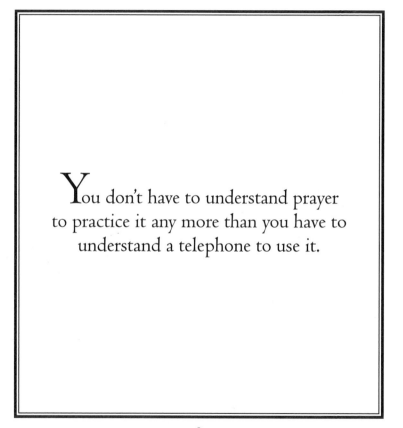

You don't have to understand prayer to practice it any more than you have to understand a telephone to use it.

Not to pray is an act of self-robbery.

We are growing in prayer as our
praying becomes an habitual attitude
rather than occasional acts.

Prayer is a privilege, not a duty;
not a burden to be borne, but a
blessing to receive.

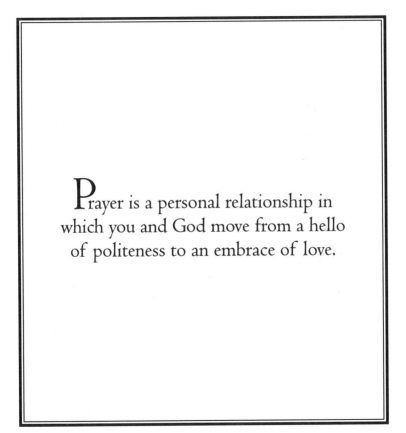

Prayer is a personal relationship in which you and God move from a hello of politeness to an embrace of love.

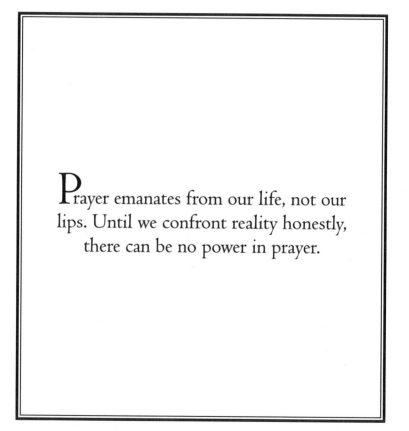

Prayer emanates from our life, not our lips. Until we confront reality honestly, there can be no power in prayer.

Would you like a daily friendship
with God? Then pray.

If your life is characterized by
practical efficiency and spiritual
shallowness, the reason may be your
lack of discipline in prayer.

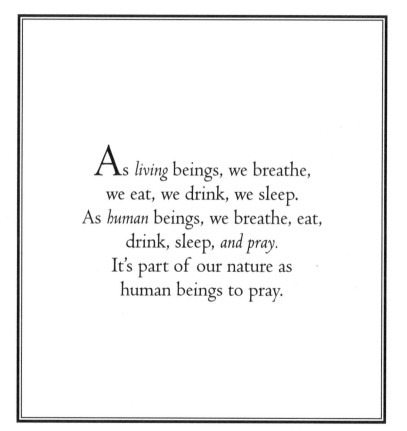

As *living* beings, we breathe,
we eat, we drink, we sleep.
As *human* beings, we breathe, eat,
drink, sleep, *and pray.*
It's part of our nature as
human beings to pray.

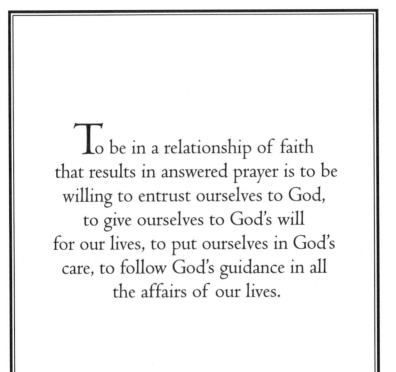

To be in a relationship of faith
that results in answered prayer is to be
willing to entrust ourselves to God,
to give ourselves to God's will
for our lives, to put ourselves in God's
care, to follow God's guidance in all
the affairs of our lives.

A foundation for prayer:
God is good, God cares, and
God wants us to communicate
with him.

———

Why do we neglect our noblest
gift—the capacity to pray?

Be patient with yourself
and your spiritual growth;
God is patient with you.

All the gifts we receive in prayer
are incidental and secondary to
God's gift of himself.

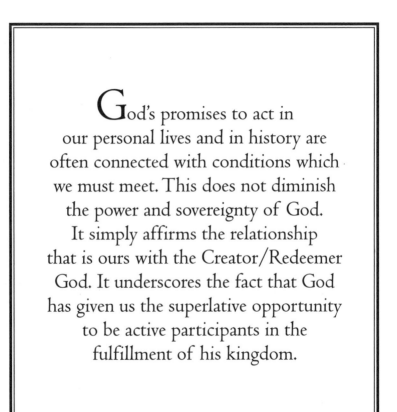

God's promises to act in
our personal lives and in history are
often connected with conditions which
we must meet. This does not diminish
the power and sovereignty of God.
It simply affirms the relationship
that is ours with the Creator/Redeemer
God. It underscores the fact that God
has given us the superlative opportunity
to be active participants in the
fulfillment of his kingdom.

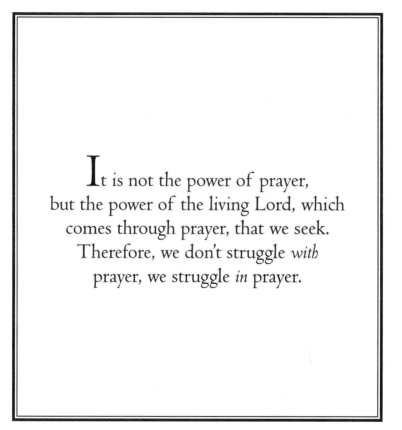

It is not the power of prayer,
but the power of the living Lord, which
comes through prayer, that we seek.
Therefore, we don't struggle *with*
prayer, we struggle *in* prayer.

It is a mystery, yet scripture
and Christian history offer
some convincing evidence that God
is as dependent upon our praying
as he is upon our acting.

It is at the heart of prayer to know
that God loves us and that we are heard
by Divine Love.

Jesus said, "I no longer call you
servants, I call you friends."
We appropriate his offer
of friendship through prayer.

———

To be heard by God
is an almost incomprehensible grace.
Equally amazing is that God not only
hears, God answers.

If God is like a father,
then communication directly or
indirectly must be at the heart
of our relationship.

In our relationship with God,
we have no rights;
it is a relationship of grace.

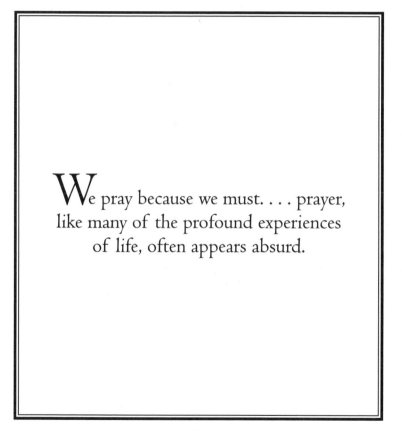

We pray because we must. . . . prayer,
like many of the profound experiences
of life, often appears absurd.

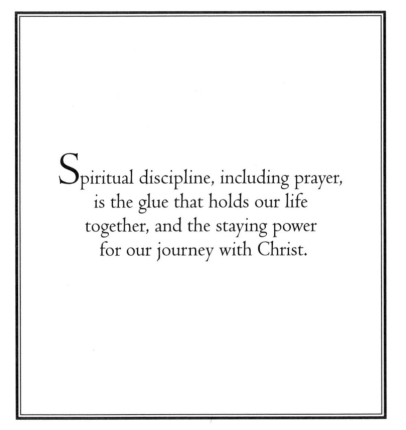

Spiritual discipline, including prayer, is the glue that holds our life together, and the staying power for our journey with Christ.

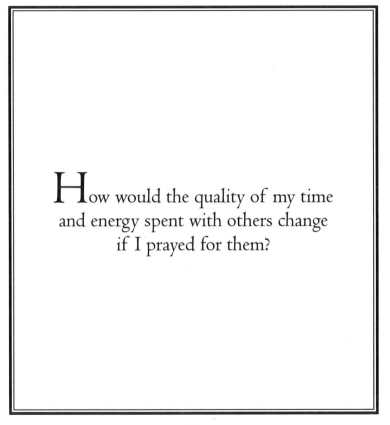

How would the quality of my time
and energy spent with others change
if I prayed for them?

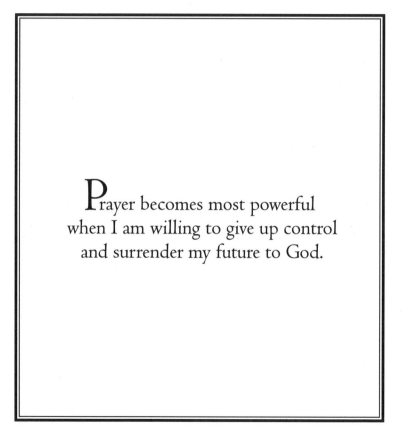

Prayer becomes most powerful
when I am willing to give up control
and surrender my future to God.

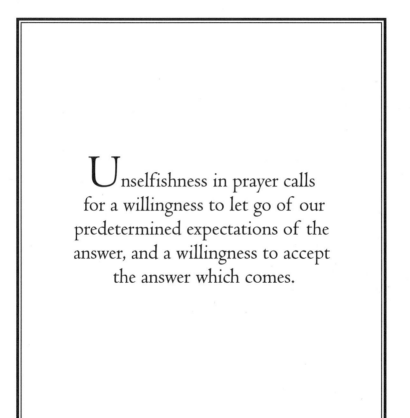

Unselfishness in prayer calls
for a willingness to let go of our
predetermined expectations of the
answer, and a willingness to accept
the answer which comes.

There is mystery in pain.
We should not hesitate to affirm that
God wills physical as well as
spiritual wholeness, . . . Yet, Christians
know pain and infirmity from which
they're not delivered. The lesson is clear:
the goal of our praying is not
primarily deliverance from pain and
suffering, but that . . . God's purposes
shall be accomplished, that Christ's
sufficient grace shall be realized.

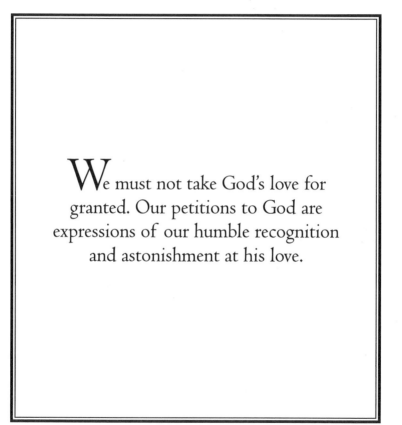

We must not take God's love for granted. Our petitions to God are expressions of our humble recognition and astonishment at his love.

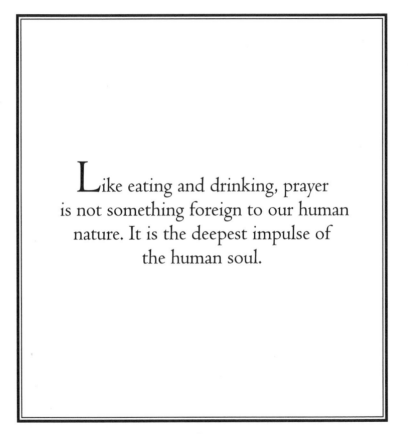

Like eating and drinking, prayer
is not something foreign to our human
nature. It is the deepest impulse of
the human soul.

Too often we add more limits to prayer than God does. God's answers to prayer are always better than our asking, and God is always more ready to hear than we are to pray.

In relationship with God, change is not only possible, it is inevitable.

God's nearness makes
all conversation with God intimate.

Things happen when we pray
that do not happen if we don't pray.

All the resources of God are available to those who will enter into a praying relationship with God.

———

God's will will not take us where God's grace will not sustain us.

Instead of being a comforting retreat
from the world, prayer becomes a
battleground where we wrestle
with what it means to live God's life
in the world.

How we think and feel
about God in relation to the tragic
dimension of our life, our pain and
suffering, shapes our whole life,
certainly our praying. . . . If we will
remember that life isn't God, then we
can affirm that though life isn't fair,
God is good. God uses the
circumstances of life to test and
shape us. Prayer also becomes a testing,
a testing of our relationship to God:
to what degree do we trust God?
How willing are we to put our lives
in God's hands?

We're often called to be
our intercession. We pray for
the hungry. God responds, "I will
answer your prayer. What will
you do for the hungry?" We pray
for the lonely, and God says,
"I hear you. What will you be for
the lonely?" We pray for peace
in the world, and God answers, "Peace
is my dream and peace begins with
you. How will you be a peacemaker?"

Prayer, especially intercession,
is an expression of our greatest love.
Instead of keeping pain
away from us, loving prayer leads us
into the suffering of God and
of others. The deeper our love of God,
the deeper our love of others.
The deeper our love of others,
the more we will suffer. The more we
suffer, the more we will pray.

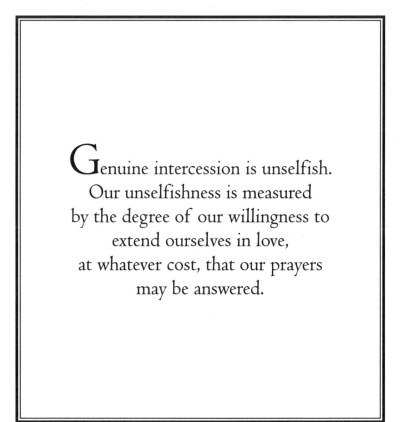

Genuine intercession is unselfish.
Our unselfishness is measured
by the degree of our willingness to
extend ourselves in love,
at whatever cost, that our prayers
may be answered.

Adoration and praise make one movement in prayer. We adore God for who God is; we praise God for what God is doing.

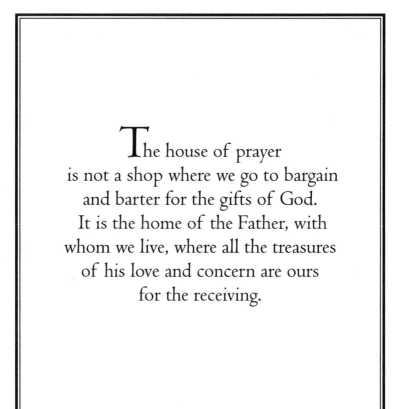

The house of prayer
is not a shop where we go to bargain
and barter for the gifts of God.
It is the home of the Father, with
whom we live, where all the treasures
of his love and concern are ours
for the receiving.

Abiding in Christ, allowing his Spirit
to live in us, is our source of power.

———

Everything that happens to us is not
God's will, but there is a will of God
in everything that happens.

As we hold our longings, questions, concerns, and desires up to God in prayer, we begin to see ourselves in the perspective of our relationship to God and others.

———

The dominant desires of our lives are the petitions of our prayers.

God sees us as we are, and God sees us more clearly and completely than we see ourselves. One of the purposes of confession is to practice seeing ourselves as God sees us.

Confession opens the door to
communion. Sin brings separation,
estrangement; forgiveness brings
reconciliation, togetherness.
Sin, then, is a barrier to communion.
Confession removes the barrier.
We come to God as we are, receive his
forgiveness which makes us feel clean,
and enter into communion with him.

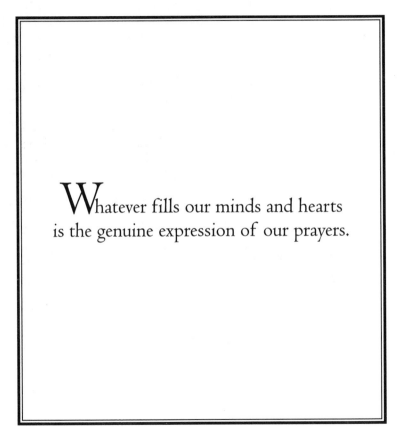

Whatever fills our minds and hearts
is the genuine expression of our prayers.

There is something demonic as well as holy in the dynamic possibilities of our desires. It is true that we usually get that upon which we set our hearts.

To pray is to stand before God "with a mind in the heart." . . . We do not come to God with our feelings here, our thoughts there, our longings hither, and our fleshly and emotional passions yonder. We come as one, integrated, our total being drawn as steel to a magnet into the sphere of our heart—to our center where the Spirit meets us.

We seek the Lord because he can be found. We thirst because God alone can and does cool our parched spiritual tongues. We hunger because God offers himself as the bread of life which alone can nourish our famished souls.

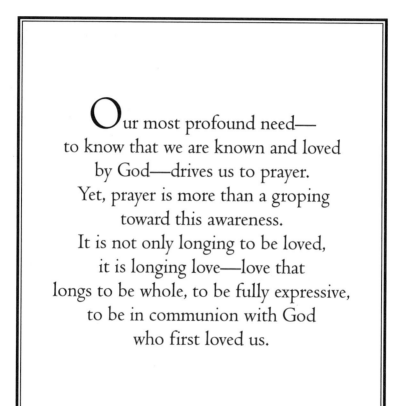

Our most profound need—
to know that we are known and loved
by God—drives us to prayer.
Yet, prayer is more than a groping
toward this awareness.
It is not only longing to be loved,
it is longing love—love that
longs to be whole, to be fully expressive,
to be in communion with God
who first loved us.

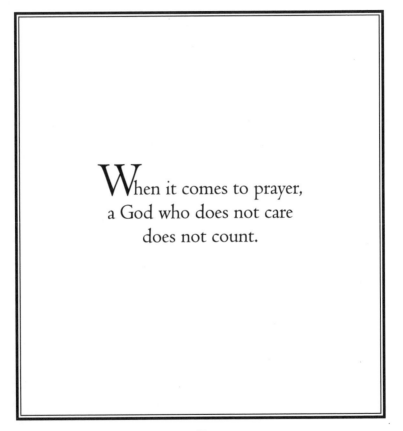

When it comes to prayer,
a God who does not care
does not count.

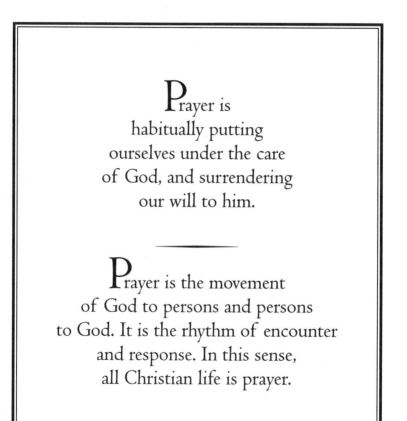

Prayer is
habitually putting
ourselves under the care
of God, and surrendering
our will to him.

Prayer is the movement
of God to persons and persons
to God. It is the rhythm of encounter
and response. In this sense,
all Christian life is prayer.

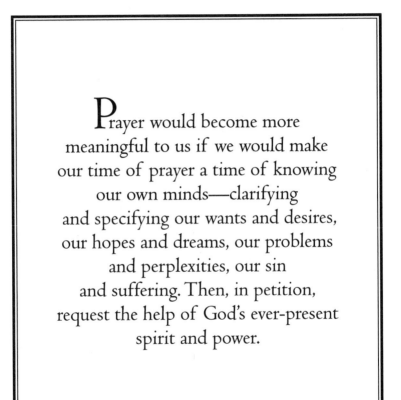

Prayer would become more
meaningful to us if we would make
our time of prayer a time of knowing
our own minds—clarifying
and specifying our wants and desires,
our hopes and dreams, our problems
and perplexities, our sin
and suffering. Then, in petition,
request the help of God's ever-present
spirit and power.

When we pray sincerely
and earnestly for others, we become
unselfish. The blessing of the other
person or situation for which we
are praying becomes our dominant
desire. This clears a channel through
which we move in service to others,
or through which God moves directly.

When we consciously seek
to relate a person whom we meet
to God, power is released about which
we know little, but which can make
a significant difference in that
person's life. Aside from that,
it will also make a tremendous
difference in our lives.

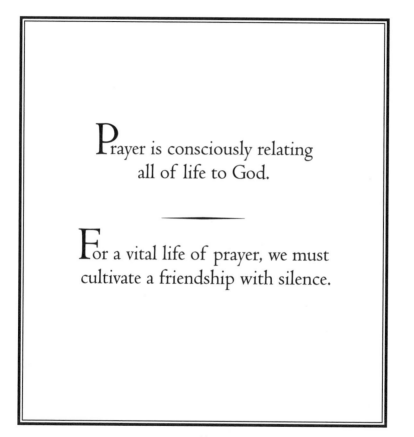

Prayer is consciously relating
all of life to God.

For a vital life of prayer, we must
cultivate a friendship with silence.

We don't stumble into a life of prayer. It comes from the deep desire to see God more clearly, to love God more dearly, and follow God more nearly.

Prayer is not my idea; it is God's idea.

This is at the heart of praying
without ceasing: being attentive
and attending to what we see.
It is only as we go beyond looking
to seeing that we can consciously relate
all of life to God.

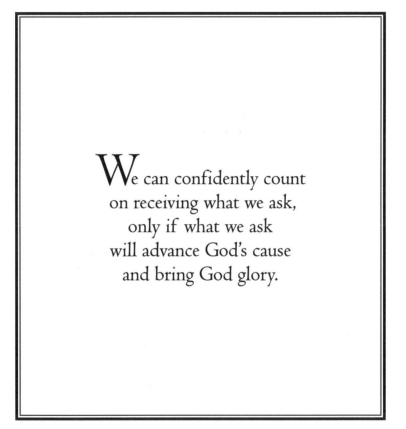

We can confidently count
on receiving what we ask,
only if what we ask
will advance God's cause
and bring God glory.

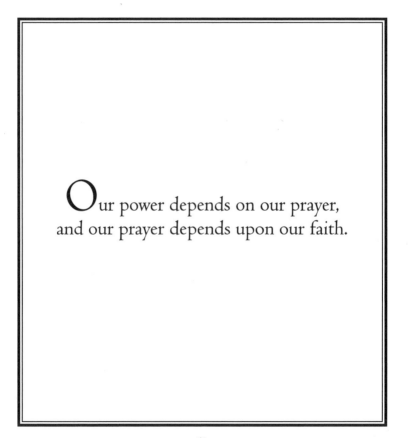

Our power depends on our prayer,
and our prayer depends upon our faith.

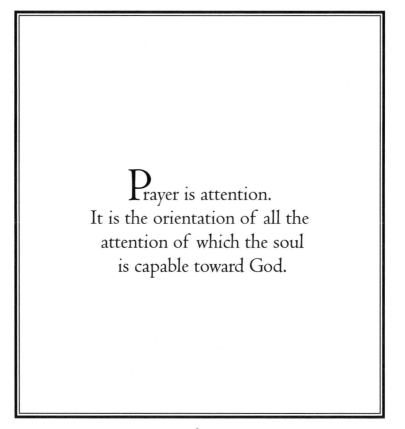

Prayer is attention.
It is the orientation of all the
attention of which the soul
is capable toward God.

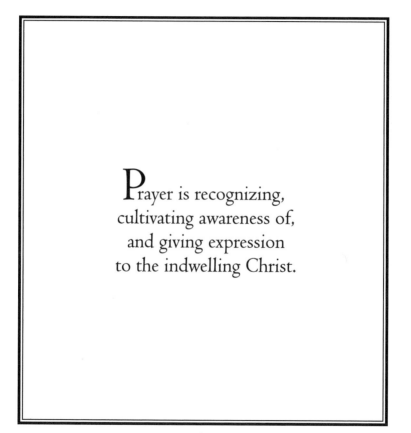

Prayer is recognizing,
cultivating awareness of,
and giving expression
to the indwelling Christ.

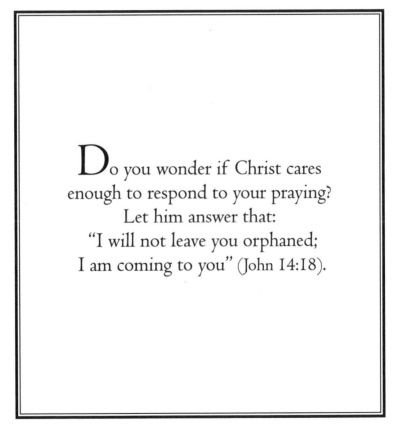

Do you wonder if Christ cares
enough to respond to your praying?
Let him answer that:
"I will not leave you orphaned;
I am coming to you" (John 14:18).

Childish praying is always asking.
Childlike praying is intent on
relationship—being with the Father
and receiving the Father's love.

When we pray, we create
a welcome for God and a response
to God's welcome.

There are three essential ingredients
to welcoming God and responding
to God's welcome:
1) Openness—expectancy and
readiness. We expect to be with God;
we're ready for God to be with us
however God pleases.
2) Stillness—settling down
in quietness, pulling in the reins of our
thoughts and feelings to seek
a centeredness.
3) Waiting—not anticipating,
not forcing, we wait to welcome
the One we trust.

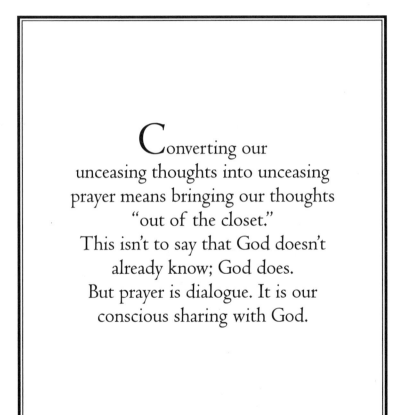

Converting our unceasing thoughts into unceasing prayer means bringing our thoughts "out of the closet."
This isn't to say that God doesn't already know; God does.
But prayer is dialogue. It is our conscious sharing with God.

A person who prays is a person standing with open arms to embrace the world and respond to all that is with the love of God.

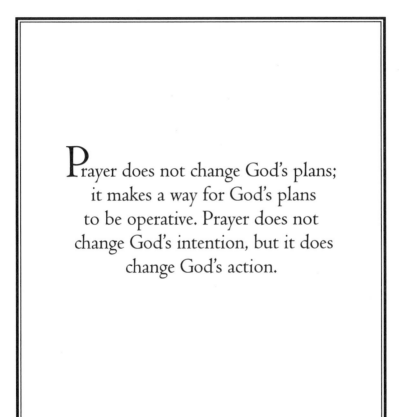

Prayer does not change God's plans;
it makes a way for God's plans
to be operative. Prayer does not
change God's intention, but it does
change God's action.

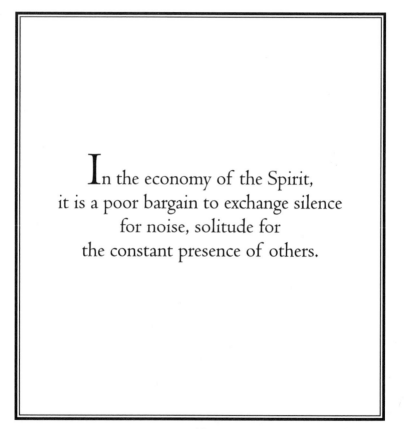

In the economy of the Spirit,
it is a poor bargain to exchange silence
for noise, solitude for
the constant presence of others.

God does not need to hear
our verbal words to hear
our prayers. Silence, where thinking is
centered and attention is focused,
may provide our deepest periods
of prayer.

The purpose of silence is
not just quietness but to enable us
to listen. Solitude that is a spiritual
discipline is not simply refraining
from talk; it is listening to God.

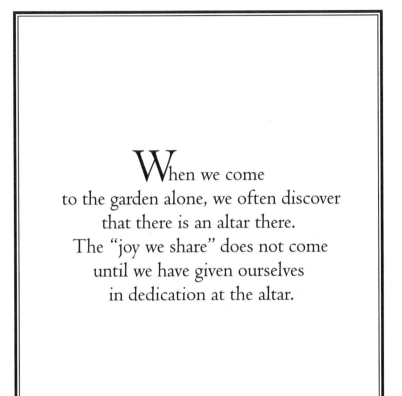

When we come
to the garden alone, we often discover
that there is an altar there.
The "joy we share" does not come
until we have given ourselves
in dedication at the altar.

What if God is as dependent upon
our praying as he is upon our acting?
What if there are some things God
either cannot or will not do until
and unless we pray?

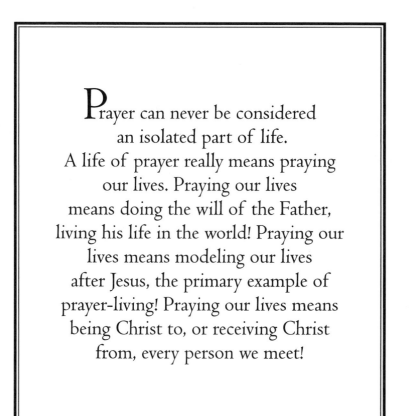

Prayer can never be considered
an isolated part of life.
A life of prayer really means praying
our lives. Praying our lives
means doing the will of the Father,
living his life in the world! Praying our
lives means modeling our lives
after Jesus, the primary example of
prayer-living! Praying our lives means
being Christ to, or receiving Christ
from, every person we meet!

There is a place in prayer for a kind
of holy anger.

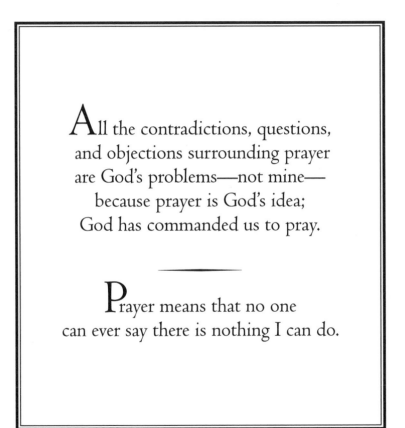

All the contradictions, questions,
and objections surrounding prayer
are God's problems—not mine—
because prayer is God's idea;
God has commanded us to pray.

Prayer means that no one
can ever say there is nothing I can do.

D o you wonder
if God hears and answers prayer?
Let God answer that:
"Before they call I will answer, while
they are yet speaking I will hear"
(Isaiah 65:24).

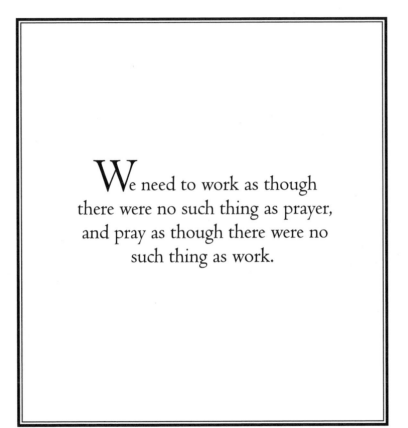

We need to work as though there were no such thing as prayer, and pray as though there were no such thing as work.

Our petitions and intercessions
are effective and powerful when
they are concrete expressions of our
trust in the goodness
and love of God. If we trust God's
goodness and love, we
can confidently put ourselves and
others in God's hands.

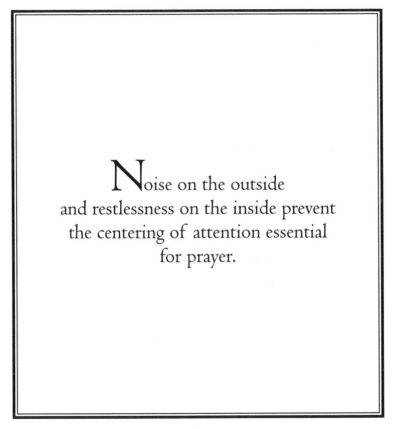

Noise on the outside
and restlessness on the inside prevent
the centering of attention essential
for prayer.

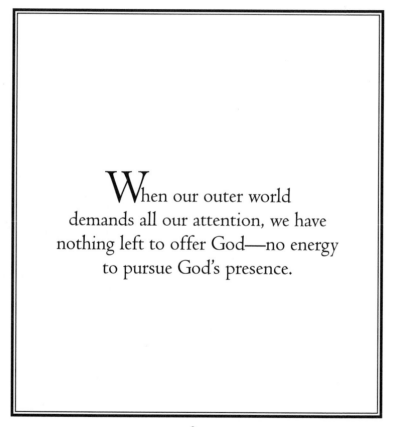

When our outer world
demands all our attention, we have
nothing left to offer God—no energy
to pursue God's presence.

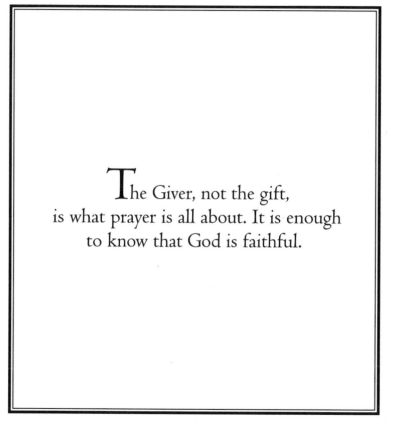

The Giver, not the gift,
is what prayer is all about. It is enough
to know that God is faithful.

A relationship has not come
to maturity until both persons
are capable and comfortable in being
silent with one another.
Such is our relationship with God
in prayer.

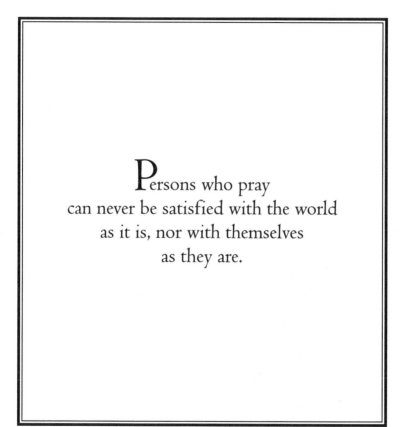

Persons who pray
can never be satisfied with the world
as it is, nor with themselves
as they are.

In prayer, we seek the joy
of relationship with God,
but more, the transformation that only
God can work in us.

There is no such thing as a part-time
Christian. There should be no such
thing as part-time praying.

The law of prayer is this: willingness to let go of self and live wholly for God. Pay attention to this law, and method will take care of itself.

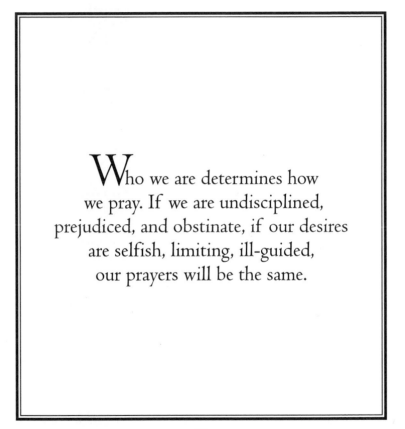

Who we are determines how
we pray. If we are undisciplined,
prejudiced, and obstinate, if our desires
are selfish, limiting, ill-guided,
our prayers will be the same.

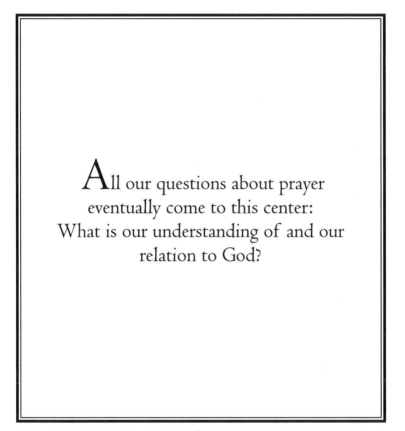

All our questions about prayer
eventually come to this center:
What is our understanding of and our
relation to God?

Prayer that changes the persons who pray and the world in which they live demands our total self in discipline, and our complete surrender to God.

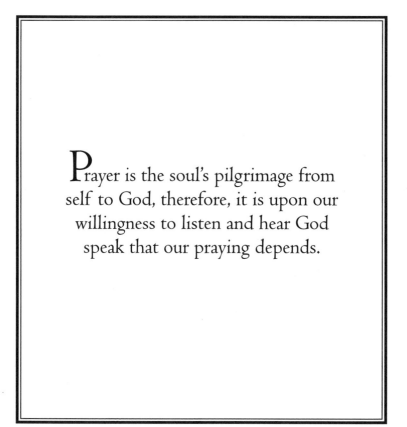

Prayer is the soul's pilgrimage from self to God, therefore, it is upon our willingness to listen and hear God speak that our praying depends.

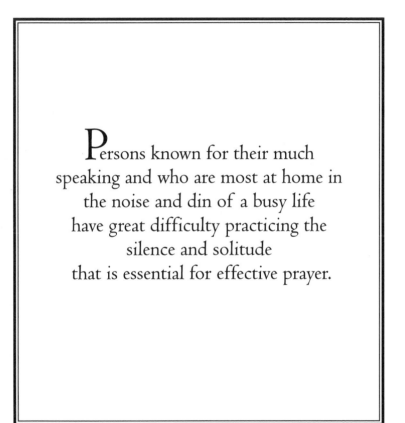

Persons known for their much
speaking and who are most at home in
the noise and din of a busy life
have great difficulty practicing the
silence and solitude
that is essential for effective prayer.

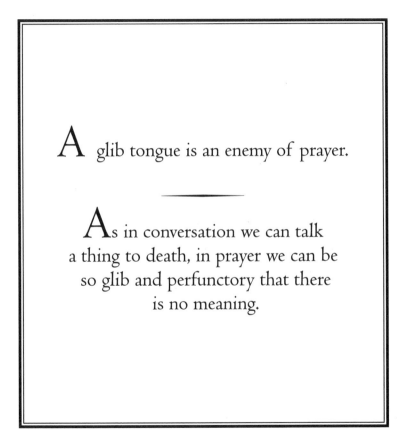

A glib tongue is an enemy of prayer.

———

As in conversation we can talk
a thing to death, in prayer we can be
so glib and perfunctory that there
is no meaning.

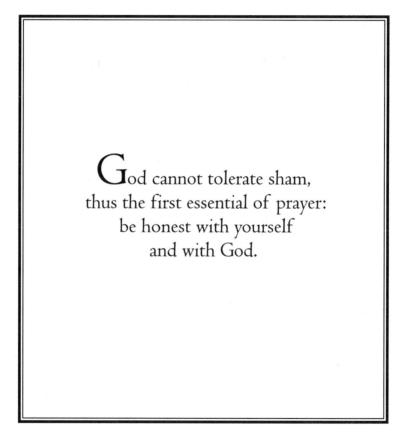

God cannot tolerate sham,
thus the first essential of prayer:
be honest with yourself
and with God.

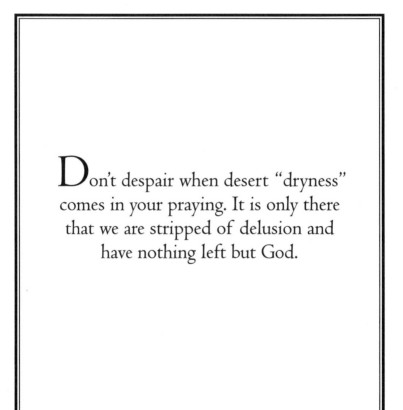

Don't despair when desert "dryness"
comes in your praying. It is only there
that we are stripped of delusion and
have nothing left but God.

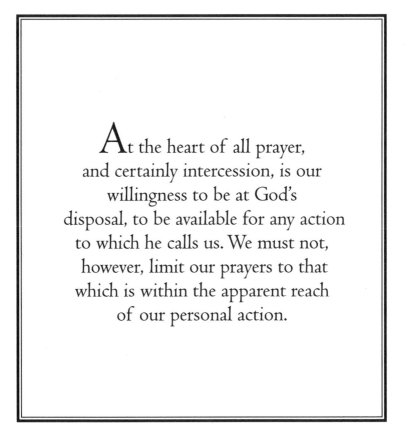

At the heart of all prayer,
and certainly intercession, is our
willingness to be at God's
disposal, to be available for any action
to which he calls us. We must not,
however, limit our prayers to that
which is within the apparent reach
of our personal action.

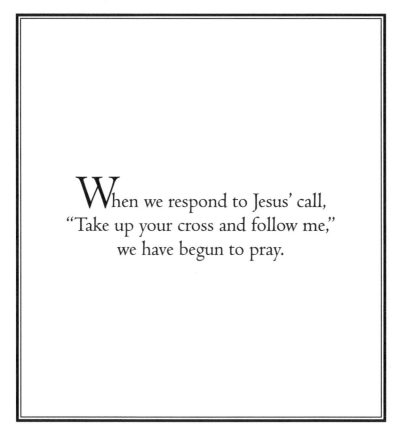

When we respond to Jesus' call,
"Take up your cross and follow me,"
we have begun to pray.

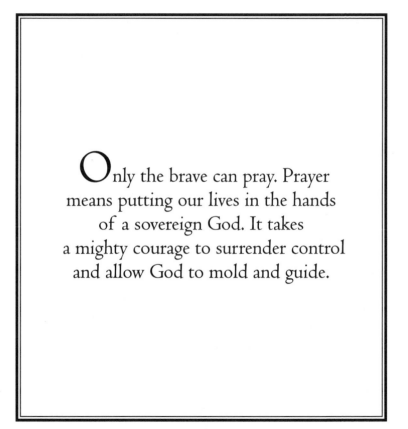

Only the brave can pray. Prayer
means putting our lives in the hands
of a sovereign God. It takes
a mighty courage to surrender control
and allow God to mold and guide.

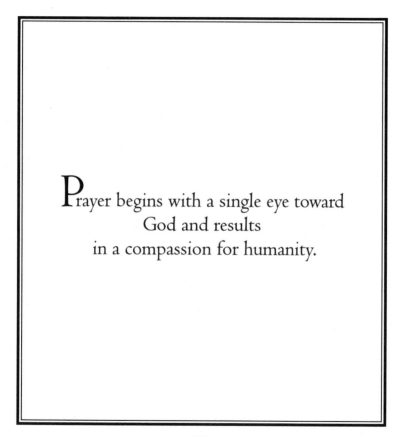

Prayer begins with a single eye toward
God and results
in a compassion for humanity.

Prayer is a death-process.
It is dying to our lower self and
coming alive to God.
We put self-will, self-control,
and self-centeredness to death
that Christ may work and reign.

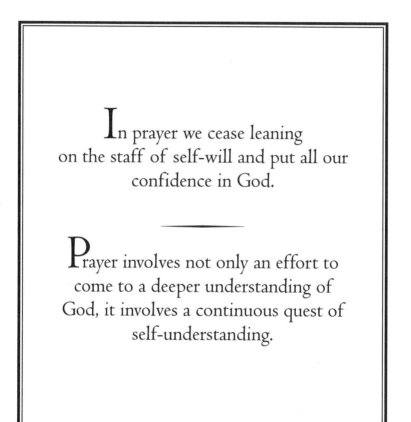

In prayer we cease leaning
on the staff of self-will and put all our
confidence in God.

—————

Prayer involves not only an effort to
come to a deeper understanding of
God, it involves a continuous quest of
self-understanding.

The sense of our helplessness
becomes the soul of our intercession.
Witness is piled upon witness,
highlighting the redemptive power
of intercession which flows from
persons who know how limited, how
utterly insufficient they are to meet
the needs of those they love.

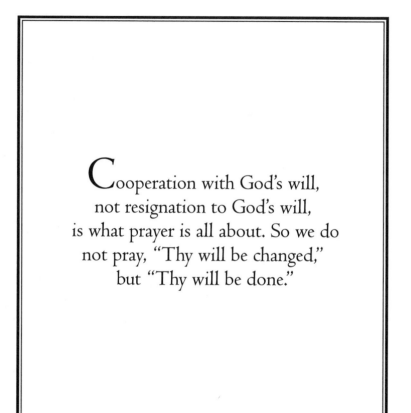

Cooperation with God's will,
not resignation to God's will,
is what prayer is all about. So we do
not pray, "Thy will be changed,"
but "Thy will be done."

We can be so busy talking
to God that we never hear God speak.

―――――――

When you don't want to pray,
pray more.

We take a giant step forward
in our praying when we move from
seeking God to realizing that God
is seeking us.

Praying that God will
substitute our wish for his plan
is not only presumptuous,
it is dumb.

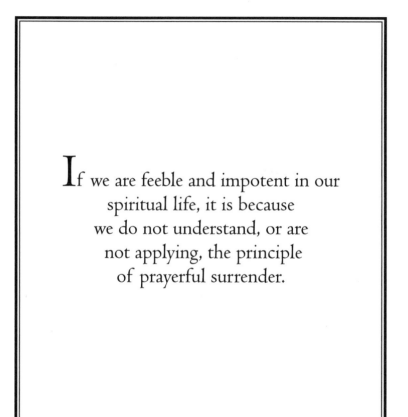

If we are feeble and impotent in our
spiritual life, it is because
we do not understand, or are
not applying, the principle
of prayerful surrender.

Neither work nor prayer can take
the place of the other.

It is easy to memorize the
Lord's Prayer but very difficult to learn
it by heart.

Saying much may be praying least.

―――――――

To deny our tendency to pray
is to rob ourselves of the nourishment
our souls need to thrive in relation
to Christ.

There is a sense in which answer
to prayer is always certain.
Even when God cannot answer
affirmatively a person's petition, he can
answer the person. If God cannot
answer the petition and change
the circumstances, he supplies sufficient
power to overcome them.
God answers either the petition
or the person.

One of the most formidable enemies
of prayer is self-deception.

In prayer, we do not seek a mystical
experience; we seek repentance
and conversion.

When you pray, come to God
genuinely as you are, not as you imagine
God would want you to be.

It is when we don't feel
a need to pray that we should pray.
Praying is easy in pain or ecstasy,
but difficult on drab, ordinary days.
When spontaneity and enthusiasm
are missing, pray as an act of will.

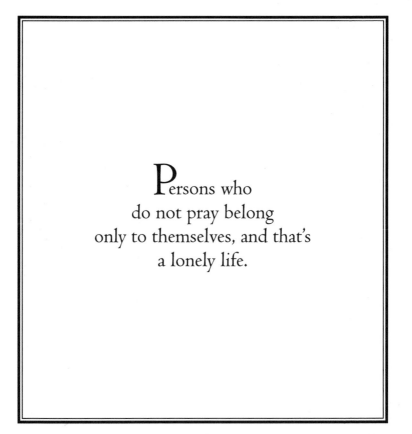

Persons who
do not pray belong
only to themselves, and that's
a lonely life.

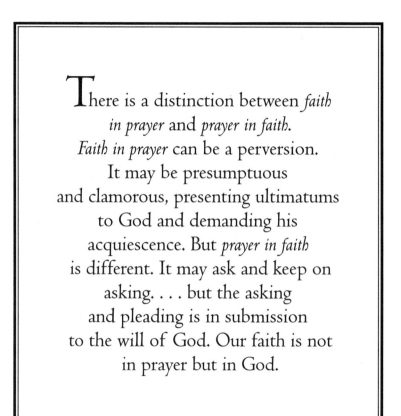

There is a distinction between *faith in prayer* and *prayer in faith*. *Faith in prayer* can be a perversion. It may be presumptuous and clamorous, presenting ultimatums to God and demanding his acquiescence. But *prayer in faith* is different. It may ask and keep on asking. . . . but the asking and pleading is in submission to the will of God. Our faith is not in prayer but in God.

*A*men is explained
in the Heidelberg Catechism to mean
"this shall truly and certainly be."
Remember this when you put
an "amen" to your prayers.

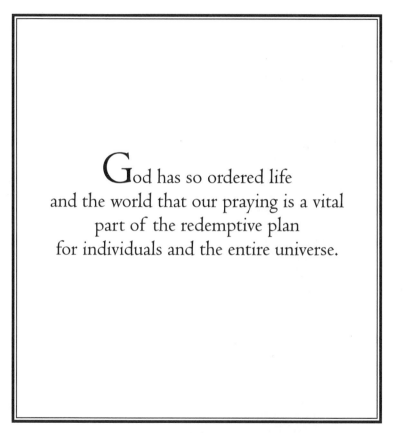

God has so ordered life
and the world that our praying is a vital
part of the redemptive plan
for individuals and the entire universe.

Intercession and petition in prayer
is the medium of exchange in God's
economy. We don't have to understand
it to practice it. We simply have
to accept the promises of God
and believe that in God's eternal
scheme of things, he has given us the
commandment to pray; and that
commandment is an opportunity,
a share in whatever it is that will bring
the will of God to the life of a person,
a situation, a relationship, or
to our own life.

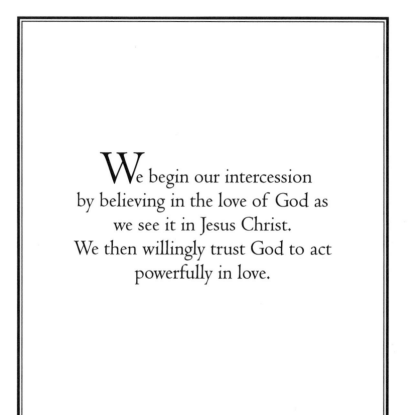

We begin our intercession
by believing in the love of God as
we see it in Jesus Christ.
We then willingly trust God to act
powerfully in love.

Intercessory prayer is love
on its knees.

It is not for lack
of understanding of prayer that we
do not pray, but for the lack
of love.

Often we do not know the needs
of those for whom we
wish to pray. We can't even find words
to express our feelings. We are silent,
but our concern is deep.
We groan within. In this spirit,
we deliberately get a vision
of the loving, caring, healing Christ,
and we bring into that awareness
those for whom we would pray, placing
them and the whole situation
in his care.

Prayer does not create
the presence of God. It makes us
aware of God's presence.

———

The heart of prayer is the soul's
response to God as fullness of love
in an act of self-surrender.

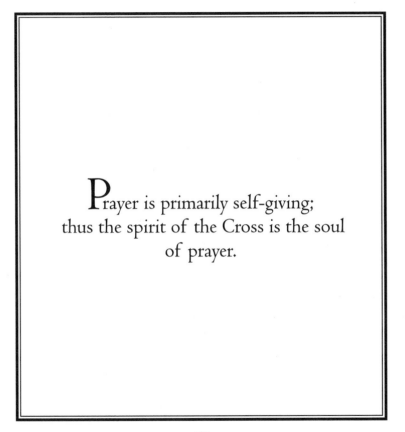

Prayer is primarily self-giving;
thus the spirit of the Cross is the soul
of prayer.

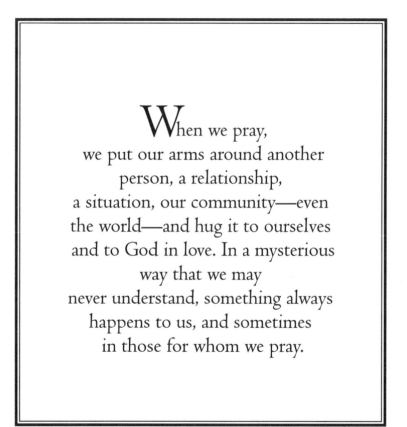

When we pray,
we put our arms around another
person, a relationship,
a situation, our community—even
the world—and hug it to ourselves
and to God in love. In a mysterious
way that we may
never understand, something always
happens to us, and sometimes
in those for whom we pray.

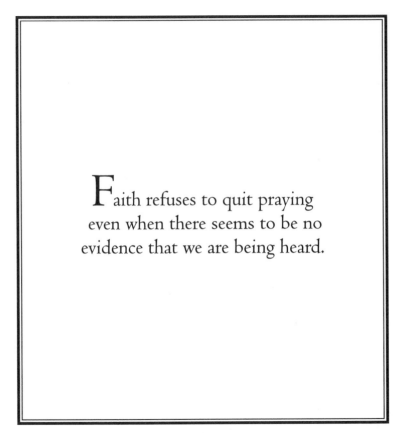

Faith refuses to quit praying
even when there seems to be no
evidence that we are being heard.

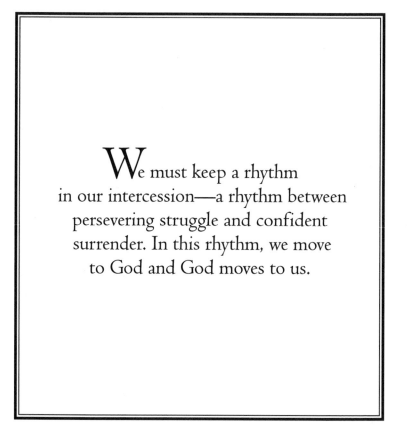

We must keep a rhythm
in our intercession—a rhythm between
persevering struggle and confident
surrender. In this rhythm, we move
to God and God moves to us.

In our helplessness we are brought
to the place where intercession
is purified and becomes powerful.
We come to the place of utter faith
in God to do what we cannot do.

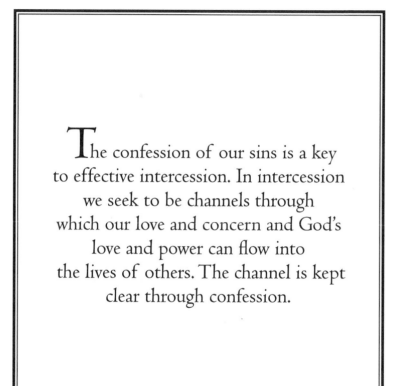

The confession of our sins is a key
to effective intercession. In intercession
we seek to be channels through
which our love and concern and God's
love and power can flow into
the lives of others. The channel is kept
clear through confession.

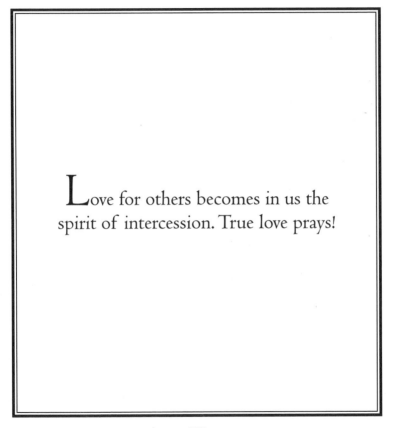

Love for others becomes in us the spirit of intercession. True love prays!

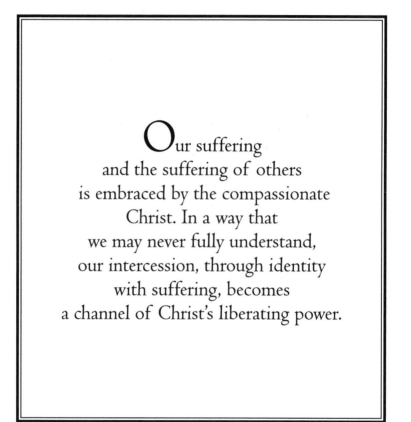

Our suffering
and the suffering of others
is embraced by the compassionate
Christ. In a way that
we may never fully understand,
our intercession, through identity
with suffering, becomes
a channel of Christ's liberating power.

If you pray when trouble comes,
does that not mean that the instinct
to pray was there all the time?
Why leave it dormant?

I doubt if there is a more powerful
way of praying for another than
to simply hold in our awareness a vision
of the person for whom we are praying
along with a vision of the loving Christ
healing and tending to the needs
of the person.

Love—longing to be loved,
but also longing love—is at the heart
of prayer. A life of prayer is a life
of desire, of yearning, of hunger,
of thirst.

To seek power in prayer is a waste
of time until you can say,
"It is no longer I who live, but it is
Christ who lives in me"
(Galatians 2:20).

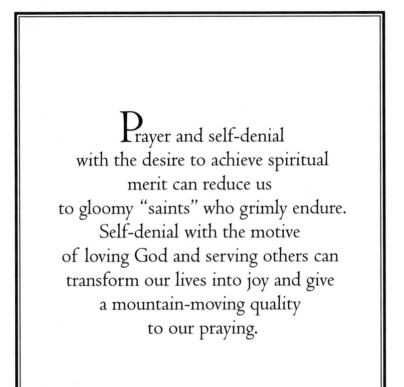

Prayer and self-denial
with the desire to achieve spiritual
merit can reduce us
to gloomy "saints" who grimly endure.
Self-denial with the motive
of loving God and serving others can
transform our lives into joy and give
a mountain-moving quality
to our praying.

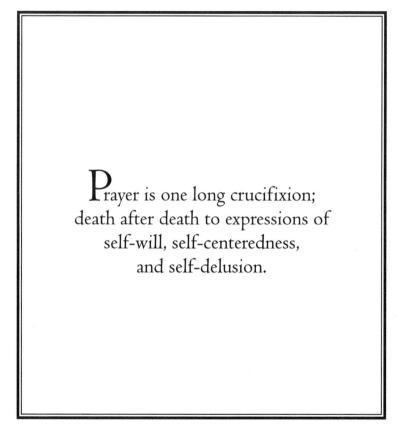

Prayer is one long crucifixion;
death after death to expressions of
self-will, self-centeredness,
and self-delusion.

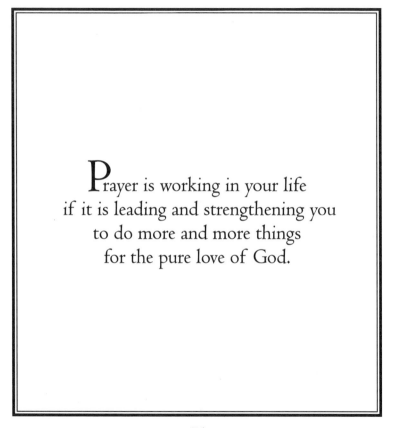

Prayer is working in your life
if it is leading and strengthening you
to do more and more things
for the pure love of God.

The most authentic and powerful
prayer comes from the person
for whom praying is as essential for
being as eating and sleeping.

Lifetime commitment
to another person in marriage,
being overwhelmed by
great music, being made speechless
by the grandeur of some piece
of nature's handiwork . . .
such experiences, along with prayer,
defy rational understanding
or description.
So we pray because we must!

No person who prays
can remain proud.

To believe that God knows and
is ordering all things for the best
doesn't cause us to cease working for
the best God has for us.
Likewise, in our praying, if it is right
to work for a certain end, isn't it just
as right to pray for that purpose?

There is power in a community
on a common journey verbalizing
their thoughts and feelings to God
in the presence of their fellow pilgrims.

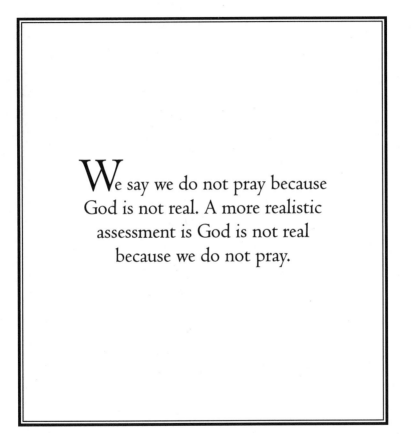

We say we do not pray because God is not real. A more realistic assessment is God is not real because we do not pray.

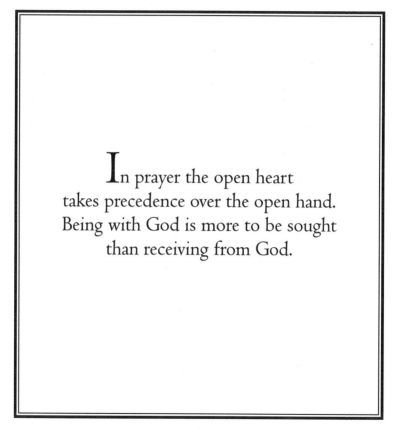

In prayer the open heart
takes precedence over the open hand.
Being with God is more to be sought
than receiving from God.

To believe that our praying makes
a difference, and to pray even when it
seems that we cannot act, is to link
ourselves with Christ in his ongoing
intercession, since "He always lives
to make intercession for *us* "
(Hebrews 7:25).

Rare is the person who
can maintain inner attentiveness
in the midst of a busy life
without being renewed by solitude.

Is the weakness of my praying
due to my doubts about the efficacy
and power of prayer?

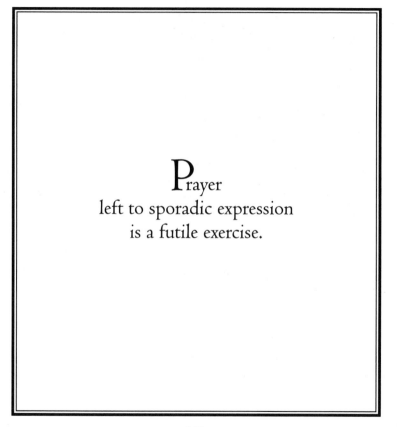

Prayer
left to sporadic expression
is a futile exercise.

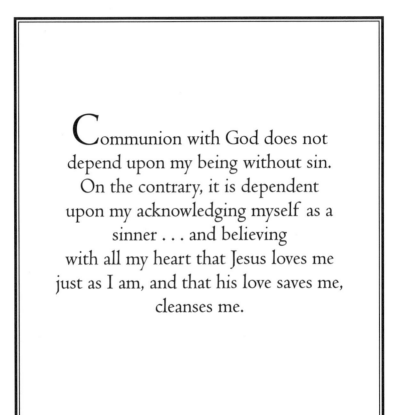

Communion with God does not
depend upon my being without sin.
On the contrary, it is dependent
upon my acknowledging myself as a
sinner . . . and believing
with all my heart that Jesus loves me
just as I am, and that his love saves me,
cleanses me.

The most active and persistent part
of our nature is our desires
and aspirations. To bring these desires
and aspirations to God in prayer and
consecration is as much God-centered
as adoration and meditation.

We can pray with confidence
if our confidence is rooted
in utter faith in God's power
and willingness to do what
we cannot do.

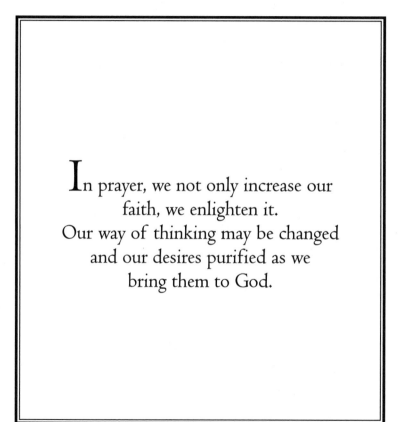

In prayer, we not only increase our
faith, we enlighten it.
Our way of thinking may be changed
and our desires purified as we
bring them to God.

Doubt conditions us
for the devil to be more effective
in our lives.

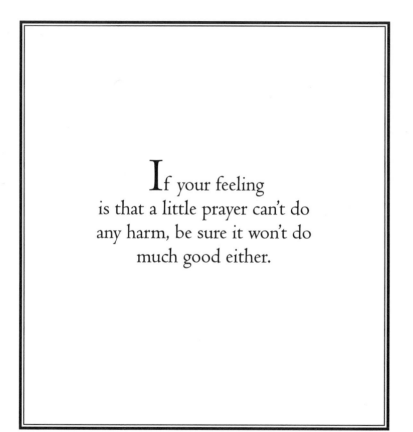

If your feeling
is that a little prayer can't do
any harm, be sure it won't do
much good either.

You cannot pray as long as you expect
the same small-mindedness
from God that you cultivate in yourself.

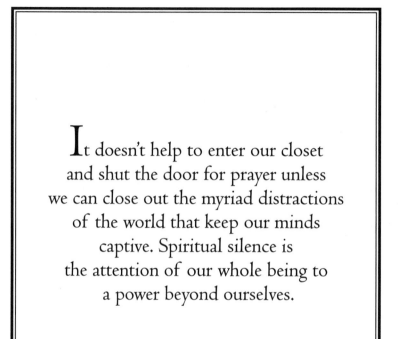

It doesn't help to enter our closet
and shut the door for prayer unless
we can close out the myriad distractions
of the world that keep our minds
captive. Spiritual silence is
the attention of our whole being to
a power beyond ourselves.

There are only two legitimate positions for a Christian: kneeling in prayer, saying, "Thy will be done"; or standing erect in readiness saying, "Here am I, send me."

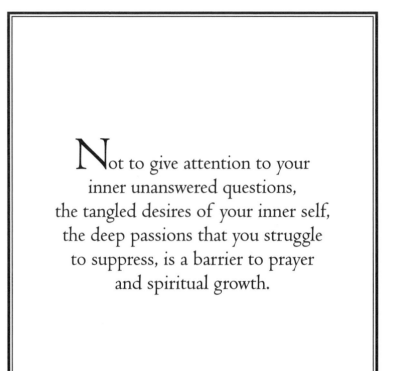

Not to give attention to your
inner unanswered questions,
the tangled desires of your inner self,
the deep passions that you struggle
to suppress, is a barrier to prayer
and spiritual growth.

Too often prayer becomes
a response to what has been, rather
than an experience of what is and what
can be. In praying about temptation
and liberation from evil, we look
to the God who calls us forward
to meet these challenges. We lay claim
to the living Christ who is
a continuing part of our experience
and yet is ahead of us,
encouraging us on.

Prayer opens our hearts.
God cannot do for a person
with a closed heart
what he can do with a person
with an open heart.

Our prayer is part of
the plan of God to work good
for those who love him.

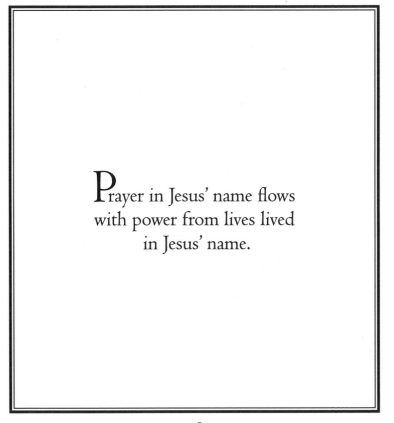

Prayer in Jesus' name flows with power from lives lived in Jesus' name.

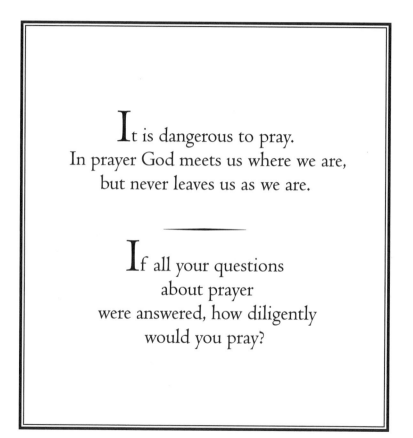

It is dangerous to pray.
In prayer God meets us where we are,
but never leaves us as we are.

_____

If all your questions
about prayer
were answered, how diligently
would you pray?

We are not aliens in the land of prayer, but natives who need to claim our citizenship rights.

God cannot give his best to us until and unless we pray.